MAINE

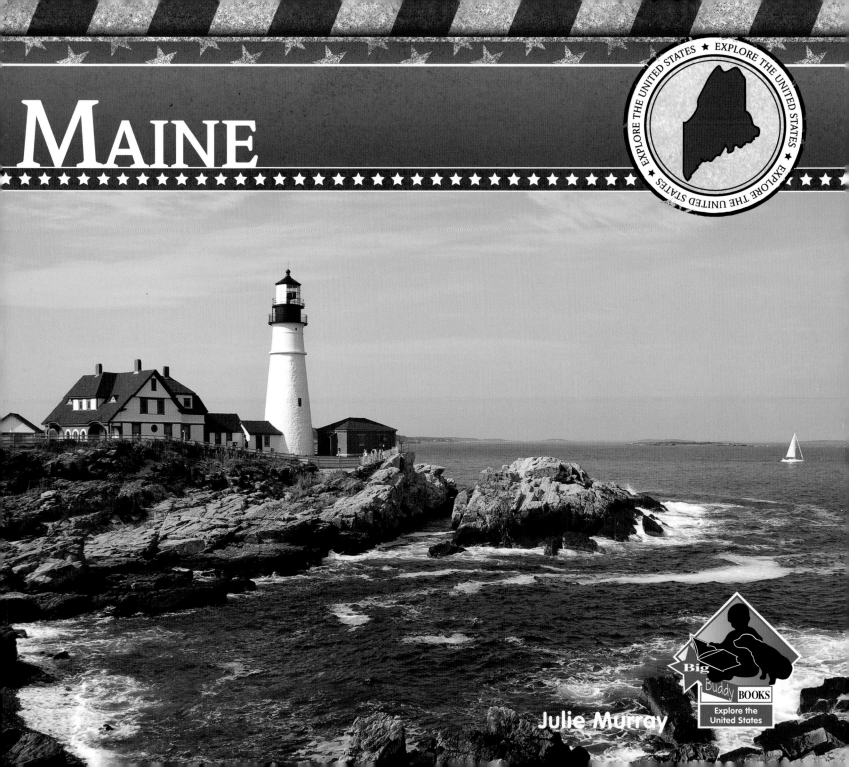

EXPLORE THE UNITED STATES ★ EXPLORE THE UNITED STATES ★ EXPLORE THE UNITED STATES ★ EXPLORE THE UNITED STATES

Julie Murray

Big Buddy BOOKS

Explore the United States

VISIT US AT
www.abdopublishing.com

Published by ABDO Publishing Company, PO Box 398166, Minneapolis, MN 55439.

Copyright © 2013 by Abdo Consulting Group, Inc. International copyrights reserved in all countries. No part of this book may be reproduced in any form without written permission from the publisher. Big Buddy Books™ is a trademark and logo of ABDO Publishing Company.

Printed in the United States of America, North Mankato, Minnesota.
042012
092012
♻ PRINTED ON RECYCLED PAPER

Coordinating Series Editor: Rochelle Baltzer
Editor: Sarah Tieck
Contributing Editors: Megan M. Gunderson, BreAnn Rumsch, Marcia Zappa
Graphic Design: Adam Craven
Cover Photograph: *Shutterstock*: Jim David.
Interior Photographs/Illustrations: *AP Photo*: Kike Calvo via AP Images (p. 19), The Portland Press Herald, Faith Cathcart (p. 27), File (p. 25), Greg Gibson (p. 25), Mark Lennihan, File (p. 23), North Wind Picture Archives via AP Images (p. 13); *Glow Images*: Stephen St. John/National Geographic Image Collection (p. 26); *iStockphoto*: ©iStockphoto.com/apelletr (p. 17), ©iStockphoto.com/judburkett (p. 17), ©iStockphoto.com/mzurawski (p. 30), ©iStockphoto.com/PictureLake (p. 29), ©iStockphoto.com/DenisTangneyJr (pp. 9, 11), ©iStockphoto.com/TVAllen_CDI (p. 26), ©iStockphoto.com/KenWiedemann (p. 9); *Shutterstock*: 9246263575 (p. 27); Steve Byland (p. 30), Brittany Courville (p. 5), Mariusz S. Jurgielewicz (p. 30), Phillip Lange (p. 30), Doug Lemke (p. 21), Chee-Onn Leong (p. 9), Alberto Loyo (p. 27).

All population figures taken from the 2010 US census.

Library of Congress Cataloging-in-Publication Data

Murray, Julie, 1969-
  Maine / Julie Murray.
    p. cm. -- (Explore the United States)
  Includes bibliographical references and index.
  ISBN 978-1-61783-357-1 (alk. paper)
  1. Maine--Juvenile literature. I. Title.
  F19.3.M87 2012
  974.1--dc23
                                     2012005983

Contents

ONE NATION

The United States is a **diverse** country. It has farmland, cities, coasts, and mountains. Its people come from many different backgrounds. And, its history covers more than 200 years.

Today the country includes 50 states. Maine is one of these states. Let's learn more about Maine and its story!

Did You Know?

Maine became a state on March 15, 1820. It was the twenty-third state to join the nation.

Maine has mountains and land covered in thick forests.

5

Maine Up Close

Did You Know?

Washington DC is the US capital city. Puerto Rico is a US commonwealth. This means it is governed by its own people.

The United States has four main **regions**. Maine is in the Northeast.

Maine borders one other state. New Hampshire is southwest. The Atlantic Ocean is southeast. The country of Canada is on Maine's northern, eastern, and western borders.

Maine's total area is 33,123 square miles (85,788 sq km). About 1.3 million people live in the state.

REGIONS OF THE UNITED STATES

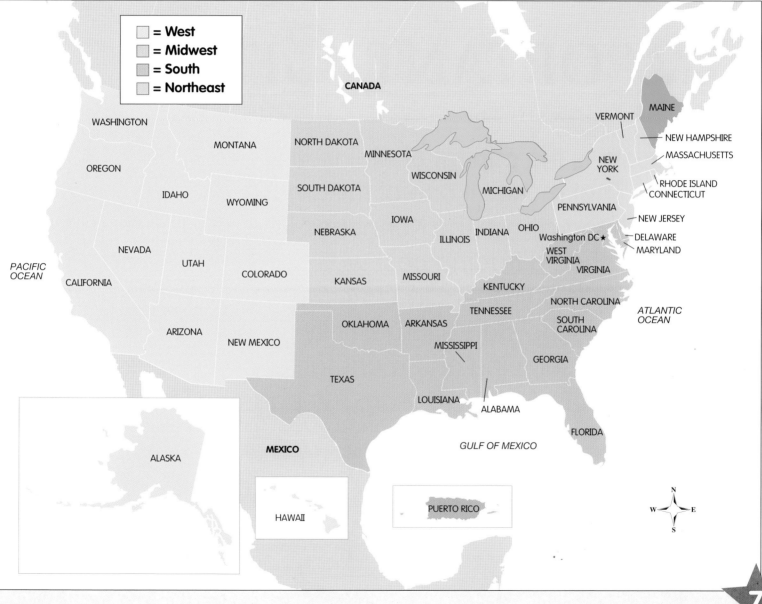

= West
= Midwest
= South
= Northeast

CANADA

WASHINGTON
OREGON
MONTANA
IDAHO
WYOMING
NEVADA
UTAH
CALIFORNIA
COLORADO
ARIZONA
NEW MEXICO

NORTH DAKOTA
MINNESOTA
SOUTH DAKOTA
WISCONSIN
NEBRASKA
IOWA
KANSAS
MISSOURI
OKLAHOMA
ARKANSAS
TEXAS
LOUISIANA

MICHIGAN
ILLINOIS
INDIANA
OHIO
KENTUCKY
TENNESSEE
MISSISSIPPI
ALABAMA
GEORGIA

MAINE
VERMONT
NEW HAMPSHIRE
MASSACHUSETTS
NEW YORK
RHODE ISLAND
CONNECTICUT
PENNSYLVANIA
NEW JERSEY
Washington DC ★
DELAWARE
WEST VIRGINIA
MARYLAND
VIRGINIA
NORTH CAROLINA
SOUTH CAROLINA
FLORIDA

PACIFIC OCEAN
ATLANTIC OCEAN
GULF OF MEXICO

ALASKA
MEXICO
HAWAII
PUERTO RICO

N
W   E
S

IMPORTANT CITIES

Augusta is the **capital** of Maine. It is home to 19,136 people. That makes it one of the smallest US capitals. It is an old port city on the Kennebec River. Its history dates to 1628, when a trading post was set up there. **Fort** Western was built there in 1754.

Portland is the state's largest city. Its population is 66,194. This shipping and manufacturing center is located on the Atlantic Ocean. It is part of a larger group of cities.

Did You Know?

Before 1832, Portland was Maine's capital.

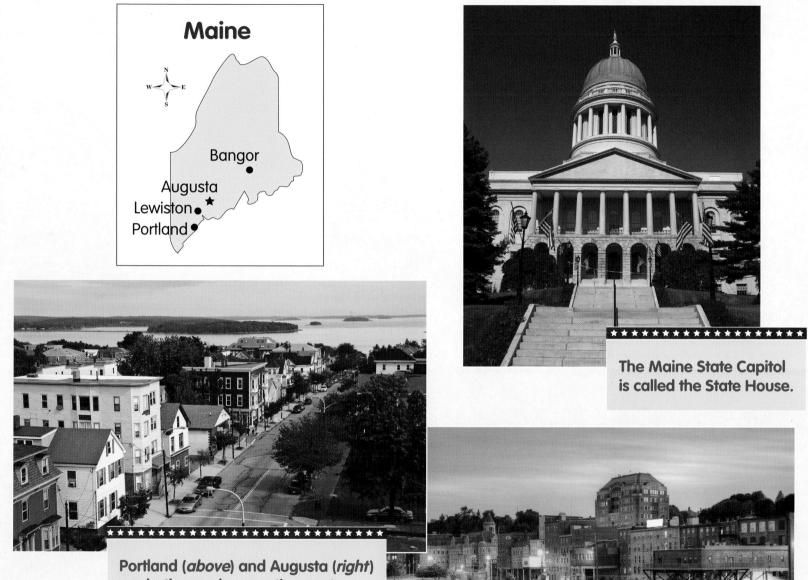

Maine

Bangor

Augusta

Lewiston

Portland

The Maine State Capitol is called the State House.

Portland (*above*) and Augusta (*right*) are both popular vacation spots.

Lewiston is the second-largest city in Maine. It is home to 36,592 people. Businesses there make cloth, footwear, and cardboard boxes. This city is also home to Bates College.

Bangor is the state's third-largest city. Its population is 33,039. It is known for manufacturing. Paper products, footwear, and electronics are made there.

Bangor is on the Penobscot River. Kenduskeag Stream (*above*) runs through the city.

Maine in History

Maine's history includes Native Americans, explorers, and war. Native Americans were the first to live in what is now Maine. They hunted, fished, and farmed there.

Explorers may have started visiting the area in the late 1400s. In the 1600s, settlements were made there. But, life was hard on the rough land. So, Maine's settlements grew more slowly than others.

French, English, and Native American people fought over the land in the 1600s and 1700s. In 1775, the **Revolutionary War** began. Soon, the United States was formed. Maine became a state in 1820.

People from Maine fought against England during the Revolutionary War. The city of Falmouth was burned and rebuilt as Portland.

Timeline

1820

On March 15, Maine became the twenty-third state.

1909

One of the first camps for girls opened on Sebago Lake. This led to the formation of the Camp Fire Girls.

1800s

West Quoddy Head Lighthouse was first built. It is one of Maine's oldest lighthouses.

1808

At age 15, Chester Greenwood made the first pair of earmuffs. Later, he had an earmuff factory in Farmington!

1873

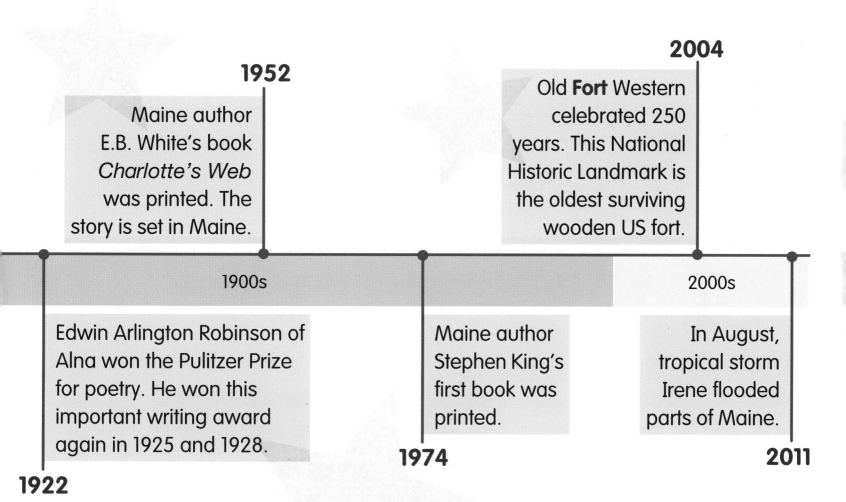

1952

Maine author E.B. White's book *Charlotte's Web* was printed. The story is set in Maine.

2004

Old **Fort** Western celebrated 250 years. This National Historic Landmark is the oldest surviving wooden US fort.

1900s

2000s

Edwin Arlington Robinson of Alna won the Pulitzer Prize for poetry. He won this important writing award again in 1925 and 1928.

Maine author Stephen King's first book was printed.

In August, tropical storm Irene flooded parts of Maine.

1922

1974

2011

Across the Land

Maine has forests, mountains, and coasts. The White Mountains cover the western part of the state. Maine is famous for its rocky coasts. They contain pink **granite**.

Many types of animals make their homes in Maine. These include moose, black bears, bobcats, and lynx. Seals, whales, and lobsters live in Maine's coastal waters.

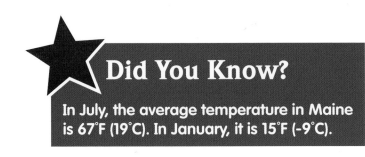

Did You Know?

In July, the average temperature in Maine is 67°F (19°C). In January, it is 15°F (-9°C).

Maine's tallest mountain peak is Mount Katahdin. It is 5,268 feet (1,606 m) high.

Strong ocean waves often crash against Maine's rocky coast.

Earning a Living

Maine used to be known mostly for making paper. Today, many people work in service jobs, such as helping visitors.

Maine has other important businesses, too. They include manufacturing, fishing, mining, forestry, and farming. These provide jobs for many people.

Did You Know?

Maine's crops include potatoes, blueberries, and apples.

People catch many types of fish off Maine's coast. They also trap lobsters.

19

Natural Wonder

Acadia National Park is on the coast of Maine. It was the first national park in the eastern United States.

Most of the park is on the rocky shores of Mount Desert Island. The park has mountains, forests, caves, cliffs, lakes, and rivers. Cadillac Mountain is there, too. It is 1,530 feet (466 m) high and made of **granite**.

People visit Acadia National Park
to hike, bike, fish, and camp.

HOMETOWN HEROES

Many famous people have lived in Maine. Author Stephen King was born in Portland in 1947. Many of his books are set in Maine.

King's first book was printed in 1974. Over the years, King has written hundreds of books and short stories. In 2003, he won a medal from the National Book Foundation. It honored King for his life's work so far.

King is known for helping others. He gives money to help Maine students attend school.

George H.W. Bush was born in Massachusetts in 1924. But, his family has spent summers in Maine for many years. They own a home in Kennebunkport.

Bush was vice president under Ronald Reagan from 1981 to 1989. He served as president from 1989 to 1993. Bush is known for his work with other countries. In 1991, he led the country during the **Persian Gulf War**.

The Bush family enjoys boating and fishing at their Kennebunkport home.

Bush was the forty-first US president.

25

Tour Book

Do you want to go to Maine? If you visit the state, here are some places to go and things to do!

 **Taste**

Have a local snack. Maine is famous for growing blueberries. Buy them, or find a farm and pick your own! Harvest time is in August.

★ See

Bird-watch at the Rachel Carson National Wildlife Refuge. It is home to more than 230 kinds of birds!

★ Go

Visit Quoddy Head State Park. It is the farthest eastern point of the United States. From the cliffs, you might see whales, seals, or bald eagles!

★ Remember

Tour the home of poet Henry Wadsworth Longfellow (*right*) in Portland. It is next door to the Maine Historical Society Museum.

★ Discover

Hike to the top of Cadillac Mountain to watch the sun rise. It is the first place you can see the sun come up in the United States during the winter months!

27

A GREAT STATE

The story of Maine is important to the United States. The people and places that make up this state offer something special to the country. Together with all the states, Maine helps make the United States great.

Maine's coasts and forests are known for their natural beauty.

Fast Facts

Date of Statehood:
March 15, 1820

Population (rank):
1,328,361
(41st most-populated state)

Total Area (rank):
33,123 square miles
(39th largest state)

Motto:
"Dirigo"
(I Direct)

Nickname:
Pine Tree State

State Capital:
Augusta

Flag:

Flower: White Pine Cone and Tassel

Postal Abbreviation:
ME

Tree: Eastern White Pine

Bird: Black-Capped Chickadee

30

Important Words

capital a city where government leaders meet.

diverse made up of things that are different from each other.

fort a building with strong walls to guard against enemies.

granite a type of very hard rock often used for building.

Persian Gulf War a war fought between Iraq and many countries, including the United States, in 1991.

region a large part of a country that is different from other parts.

Revolutionary War a war fought between England and the North American colonies from 1775 to 1783.

Web Sites

To learn more about Maine, visit ABDO Publishing Company online. Web sites about Maine are featured on our Book Links page. These links are routinely monitored and updated to provide the most current information available.

www.abdopublishing.com

Index